Original title:
The Song Remains

Copyright © 2024 Swan Charm
All rights reserved.

Author: Liina Liblikas
ISBN HARDBACK: 978-9908-1-2695-1
ISBN PAPERBACK: 978-9908-1-2696-8
ISBN EBOOK: 978-9908-1-2697-5

A Tidal Wave of Infinite Sound

A whisper glides on ocean breeze,
Carrying secrets from the deep.
Waves crash forth with mighty ease,
In melodies that cradle sleep.

Harmony in each swell and crest,
Nature sings in vibrant hue.
Rhythms pulse, our hearts attest,
To the song the waters do.

Distant drums in thunder grow,
Calling spirits to arise.
They dance upon the tidal flow,
Underneath the stormy skies.

Every drop holds ancient tales,
Of past lives washed ashore.
In their depths the voice prevails,
Echoing forevermore.

Together in this vast expanse,
Whispers weave, and spirits blend.
Lost in this enchanting dance,
To the sound, our souls will mend.

The Symphony of Enduring Echoes

In shadows where the silence stirs,
A note arises from the night.
Softly sung, it gently blurs,
The lines between the wrong and right.

Each chord, a bridge to distant lands,
Where dreams wander and hope is found.
Life's melody in timeless strands,
Calls forth the echoes all around.

In harmony, the past is heard,
With every heartbeat that we share.
The music flows, a whispered word,
Uniting hearts with tender care.

In crescendos, passions rise,
A symphony of joy and pain.
Beneath the vast and starry skies,
Our stories swell like autumn rain.

Forever bound in sound's embrace,
The echoes linger, strong and bright.
A symphony of time and space,
Guiding us toward the light.

The Slumbering Harmony of Existence

In whispers soft, the night does greet,
Stars above in silence breathe.
Each dream entwined, a path to seek,
In slumber's hush, our hearts believe.

Nature hums a gentle tune,
Crickets chirp their nightly song.
The moonlight dances through the leaves,
In timeless grace, we all belong.

A breeze caresses, tender and light,
As shadows play, and moments blend.
Together in this tranquil night,
We find the peace that time can lend.

Among the stars, our spirits soar,
A tapestry of cosmic art.
In slumber's realm, forevermore,
The harmony of life imparts.

Awake, we chase the dawn's bright glow,
Yet in our hearts, the echoes cling.
For in the night, we come to know,
Existence holds us in its wing.

Echoes of a Fading Horizon

As daylight wanes, the shadows creep,
Colors blend in twilight's embrace.
Whispers fade, like secrets deep,
In the dusk, memories trace.

Waves crash softly on the shore,
Each tide a tale of yesteryear.
The horizon calls, forevermore,
Echoes linger, sweet yet clear.

In fading light, the night unfolds,
Stars awaken from their dreams.
Stories whispered, softly told,
In silence, the world redeems.

The past a canvas, painted bright,
In shadows cast, we find our way.
With each embrace of the coming night,
We bid the sun a soft dismay.

Yet in the dark, new hopes arise,
As dawn's first light begins to sway.
The horizon shifts, a changing guise,
In echoes bold, life finds its play.

The Pulse of Forgotten Songs

In the stillness, echoes ring,
A melody of days gone by.
Forgotten songs, the heart does sing,
In whispers soft, we learn to fly.

Notes that dance on autumn's breeze,
Stories woven into the air.
With each refrain, we're brought to knees,
In harmony, our souls laid bare.

Time may fade what once was bold,
Yet in the silence, rhythms sway.
Lost tales of love and dreams untold,
Beat within us, come what may.

With every heartbeat, music lives,
A pulse that guides us through the night.
Through shadows deep, the spirit gives,
A timeless force, the strongest light.

This hand of fate, our song we claim,
In every breath, the tune remains.
The pulse of life, forever same,
In forgotten songs, love sustains.

Tapestry of Echoing Rhythms

In concert dawn, the world awakes,
Nature's beat a vibrant thread.
With every step, the earth partakes,
In woven sounds, our hearts are led.

The rivers hum a lively tune,
Mountains echo with a roar.
Every leaf sways to the moon,
In perfect sync, we all explore.

Beneath the stars, the night resounds,
With crickets chorus in the dark.
A symphony of life surrounds,
Each note a flicker, each beat a spark.

Within this tapestry we find,
The rhythm of our fleeting days.
In every heart, a song aligned,
In harmony, the music plays.

So dance we shall to life's sweet song,
In every moment, let us stir.
In echoes strong, we all belong,
A tapestry of love, a blur.

Timeless Symphonies

In the hush of twilight's glow,
Melodies drift and softly flow.
Strings weave tales of days gone by,
Resonating with the sigh.

Notes that dance on gentle air,
Whispers echo everywhere.
Chords unite both hearts and minds,
Binding souls that fate unwinds.

Each refrain a moment caught,
Binding memories once sought.
Harmony that never fades,
In the heart, it serenades.

Echoing Legacies

Lives entwined through time's own thread,
Stories linger, words unsaid.
In the shadows, echoes gleam,
Carrying forth a shared dream.

Fading faces in the mist,
But their essence can't be missed.
Each heartbeat writes a tale anew,
In the fabric, past finds hue.

Legacy in every stone,
Whispers of those now unknown.
Time stands still, yet it keeps track,
Echoes pull us, never slack.

Echoes and Eclipses

When shadows fall, the world stands still,
A cosmic dance in silent thrill.
Celestial bodies in their grace,
Painting memory's timeless face.

Echoes ring through the starlit night,
A fleeting glimpse of waning light.
Phases shift, yet love remains,
In the dark, hope still retains.

Hearts aligned in cosmic play,
Drawing near, then drifting away.
Eclipses pass, but dreams ignite,
Guided by the moon's soft light.

Fading yet Forever

In the twilight's tender glow,
Time whispers soft, yet we know.
Memories wane like the setting sun,
Yet in our hearts, they still run.

Fading colors, yet they shine,
Through the veil, they intertwine.
Moments cherished, never lost,
Love transcends the heaviest cost.

Forever held in sacred space,
Where echoes find their rightful place.
Though time may dim the brightest light,
In our souls, they burn so bright.

Echoes of Yesterday

In twilight's glow, shadows speak,
Of moments lost, of futures bleak.
Soft whispers trace the paths we tread,
Where dreams once bloomed, now echoes spread.

The laughter fades, yet still it plays,
In corridors of ancient days.
Each heartbeat echoes, faint and clear,
Resounding through the vale of years.

A photograph holds time's embrace,
Reflecting smiles, a fleeting grace.
Yet every glance, a bittersweet,
In silent halls where memories meet.

Through changing seasons, we roam wide,
With every step, old ghosts abide.
Their stories linger, sweet and raw,
In the tapestry of time's soft draw.

To honor those who came before,
We dance through shadows, evermore.
These echoes guide our hearts tonight,
As past and present intertwine in light.

Melodies of Memory

Each note a whisper, soft refrain,
In symphonies of joy and pain.
The past unfolds with every chord,
A timeless song in hearts adored.

From dusk till dawn, the music swells,
In quiet moments, silence tells.
The laughter echoes, sweetly spun,
Within the notes, we're all as one.

A distant tune reminds of grace,
In every smile, in every face.
The melody, a gentle guide,
Through realms where memories reside.

When words are lost, the song remains,
In whispered breaths, in soft refrains.
We gather close, in harmony,
Together wrapped in melody.

Each moment captured, held so dear,
In the music, we shed a tear.
As time goes by, we hold it near,
In melodies of love sincere.

Harmonies That Linger

Through tangled woods, a song does weave,
In echoes faint, we dare believe.
Each harmony a soothing balm,
That carries us in peace, so calm.

The rhythm pulses, soft and low,
In twilight's arms, our spirits grow.
With every heartbeat, notes align,
In music's grace, our souls entwine.

Faint whispers dance upon the breeze,
As nature sings, our hearts find ease.
In gentle tones, the world revolves,
In harmonies, our truth evolves.

As stars align in night's embrace,
We find ourselves in time and space.
In every chord, a promise lingers,
A gift of life in sweeted fingers.

The past, the present, all combined,
In melodies that bind our minds.
The echoes fade but never part,
For harmonies reside in heart.

Whispers Through Time

In quiet rooms, the memories fade,
Yet softly still, our hearts are swayed.
With every breath, a tale is spun,
In whispers low, our journeys run.

Across the years, a gentle breeze,
Carries words like autumn leaves.
In shadows cast by evening's glow,
We find the truths we yearn to know.

Each soft embrace, a moment shared,
In secret smiles, we're always paired.
Through trials faced and joys confined,
The whispers linger, intertwined.

As twilight falls, we'll seek the light,
In stories told, through day and night.
Across the canvas of our days,
The whispers guide us through life's maze.

In every heartbeat, time takes hold,
In whispered dreams, our lives unfold.
Though years may pass, our voices rhyme,
In echoes soft, through endless time.

The Ageless Echo of Melodies

In shadows where the soft notes play,
A haunting tune drifts far away.
Each whisper cradles timeless grace,
Embracing dreams in sweet embrace.

The strings will weave a tapestry,
Of love and loss, of you and me.
Resonance fills the open air,
As echoes linger everywhere.

From ancient hearts, the rhythms flow,
Through mountains high and valleys low.
The ageless sound forever near,
In every heart, a melody clear.

With every beat, the memories call,
The dance of life, it captivates all.
Within the echoes, time stands still,
In music's arms, we find our will.

So let us sing beneath the stars,
With joyful notes, we break the bars.
For in this sound, we are alive,
In melodies, our spirits thrive.

The Unwritten Symphony of Life

In silence waits the sweetest score,
Notes yet to come, like waves ashore.
Each heartbeat plays a hidden tune,
A melody that makes us swoon.

With every breath, potential sings,
Life's canvas stretched with vibrant wings.
We sketch our dreams with each new day,
In symphonies, we find our way.

Fleeting moments intertwine,
In chaos, beauty starts to shine.
The unwritten paths we choose to tread,
Compose a song, our spirits fed.

As seasons change, our music swells,
In laughter, tears, and whispered spells.
A harmony we craft with care,
In life's grand play, we find our share.

So let the notes cascade and flow,
An unwritten song we learn to know.
For in each life, a symphony,
Awaits to rise and set us free.

Whispers Tucked into Time's Fold

Within the corners of the night,
Whispers dance with gentle light.
Every secret softly spun,
Reveals the threads of things undone.

Time holds tales of love and loss,
Each moment etched, a sacred gloss.
In hushed tones, the echoes play,
Whispers guide us on our way.

The past entwined with present's hand,
In every heartbeat, stories stand.
We listen close to what was said,
In whispered truths, we find our thread.

Beyond the veil of years gone past,
Each whisper teaches us to last.
In silent corners, wisdom glows,
As time bestowed, the river flows.

So keep the whispers in your heart,
For every voice will play its part.
In echoes, we embrace our soul,
Tucked within time's gentle roll.

A Lyric for Every Lost Hour

When moments fade like distant stars,
A lyric lingers from afar.
Each hour past, a haunting song,
In memories, we still belong.

We seek the notes of days once shared,
In melodies, our hearts are bared.
For every loss, a tune remains,
In whispered chords of joy and pain.

The clock may tick, the sun may set,
Yet in our thoughts, we won't forget.
The lyrics written in the dark,
Illuminate each fading spark.

So let us hold the echoes tight,
In every lost hour, find the light.
For in the silence, songs arise,
A tribute to our cherished ties.

A lyric crafted from the heart,
Reminds us that we've played our part.
In every note, a story sung,
For lost hours, a new song begun.

The Heartbeat of Resilient Reverberations

In shadows cast by trials faced,
A steady pulse, a heart embraced.
Through storms that roar and winds that cry,
We rise anew, our spirits high.

From ashes cold, the fire ignites,
With every step, we claim our rights.
A dance of hope in every beat,
Together we're whole, not just complete.

With scars that tell of battles fought,
In every breath, resilience taught.
We march to drums of ancient lore,
Each heartbeat echoes, evermore.

When darkness looms and doubts arise,
Look to the stars, beyond the skies.
For in the night, our courage gleams,
We forge our paths, we chase our dreams.

In unity, our voices blend,
A symphony we shall not end.
Through every trial, our spirits sing,
A heartbeat strong, forever spring.

Echoing Dreams of a Distant Tomorrow

In twilight's glow, we dare to dream,
A world reborn, a flowing stream.
With whispers soft, the future calls,
As hope takes wing, and courage falls.

Through valleys deep and mountains high,
We stretch our hands, we aim for the sky.
In unity, our visions soar,
Together we'll reach that distant shore.

With hearts entwined, we paint the light,
A canvas bright, dispelling night.
Each brushstroke shows what we believe,
In every moment, we can achieve.

In echoes sweet, the past will fade,
As we embrace the plans we made.
With every heartbeat, dreams take flight,
In distant tomorrows, we find our light.

So let us dance in starlit haze,
Embracing hope in countless ways.
For every dream that we ignite,
Transforms the day, makes darkness bright.

Melodies Interwoven in Silence

In quietude, the world unfolds,
With whispers soft, the truth beholds.
A symphony of hearts align,
In silent chords, our spirits shine.

Threads of melody, soft and sweet,
Embrace our souls, in time we meet.
With every pause, the heartbeat's song,
In silent spaces, we belong.

The world may hush, yet we can hear,
The echoes of what we hold dear.
In stillness lies the purest grace,
A dance of light, a warm embrace.

With gentle notes, we weave our fate,
In hidden realms, we resonate.
Through every whisper, hope takes flight,
A melody in the velvet night.

So let us cherish moments rare,
In silent tunes, our dreams laid bare.
For in the quiet, love will thrive,
Interwoven threads, forever alive.

Threads of Rhythmic Eternity

In timeless dance, we find our way,
Through woven paths of night and day.
With every heartbeat, we entwine,
As rhythms pulse, our souls align.

In endless loops, the fabric spins,
Where every journey deep within begins.
With trust and hope, we seek the light,
In threads of gold that glow so bright.

Each moment shared, a tapestry,
Of laughter, tears, and memory.
With every thread, a story spun,
In rhythmic patterns, we are one.

Through valleys low and mountains steep,
In every promise, dreams we keep.
As echoes dance, our spirits soar,
In timeless threads, forevermore.

So let us weave with joy and grace,
A tapestry that time can't erase.
For in this dance, we freely flee,
In threads of rhythmic eternity.

Resonance of the Spirit.

In shadows deep, the whispers call,
A dance of light, where silence falls.
The heartbeats pulse, alive with grace,
In every breath, we find our place.

The flowing stream sings tales of old,
Of dreams once chased, of secrets told.
Each soaring note, a guiding star,
In unity, we've come so far.

Through tangled woods, the echoes roam,
A melody that calls us home.
With every step, we blend and weave,
In harmony, we dare believe.

Unseen threads connect our souls,
A song that softly takes its toll.
In every loss, there lies a gain,
A symphony born from the pain.

As twilight falls, the night awakes,
A chorus builds, our spirits break.
With every note, we rise again,
In resonant hearts, we find the zen.

Echoes of Everlasting Melodies

The dawn breaks sweet, a soft refrain,
Where glimmers dance on dew-kissed grain.
Each whisper stirs the morning light,
In every chord, the world takes flight.

Time weaves its threads through joy and pain,
In echo's grasp, we bloom and wane.
A tapestry of dreams entwined,
In melodies, our fates are aligned.

The mountains hum a timeless song,
In every note, we all belong.
With every rise and every fall,
The echoes weave through nature's call.

Like rivers flow, we bend and sway,
In harmony with night and day.
A rhythm found in moonlit skies,
In every breath, a prayer that flies.

So gather 'round, let voices soar,
In unity, we'll seek for more.
With love and hope, we dare to dream,
In echoes of an endless stream.

Whispers of Time's Endless Tune

The clock ticks soft, a gentle sound,
In moments lost, where dreams abound.
Each heartbeat whispers truths untold,
In time's embrace, we grow bold.

Beneath the stars, the secrets sigh,
That float upon an endless sky.
With every dawn, we start anew,
In whispers shared between the few.

Nature hums a soothing song,
In echoes where our hearts belong.
The rustling leaves, they sing our fate,
In every breath, we learn to wait.

In twilight's glow, the world feels near,
With every sound, the past is clear.
Each note a story, softly spun,
Through time's embrace, we are all one.

As shadows blend with light's embrace,
We find our path, we find our grace.
In whispers soft, we find our tune,
Together, we write our own monsoon.

Harmonies that Defy Erasure

In every note, a memory stays,
Through nights of calm and sunlit days.
The pulse of life, a vibrant breeze,
In harmony, we find our keys.

The echoes ring through ages past,
Each melody, a shadow cast.
In whispered tones, we break the chains,
Through song and rhythm, love remains.

Stronger now, the chorus climbs,
Beyond the bounds of space and time.
In every heart, a song resides,
With harmonies the world provides.

Though seasons change, the music flows,
In light and dark, our spirit grows.
Each whispered tale, a gentle trace,
In every song, we find our grace.

So let the world hear our refrain,
Through joy and sorrow, love remains.
In unity, our voices rise,
In harmonies that touch the skies.

Cadence of Unfading Notes

In the silence, whispers rise,
Carried softly through the skies.
Each note dances, pure and free,
An echo of eternity.

Fingers trace the strings of time,
Creating rhythms, pure and prime.
In every heart, a pulse remains,
Bound by love, through joy and pains.

Above the clouds, the stars align,
Filling voids with every sign.
A symphony of all we share,
In every breath, in every prayer.

Harmonies from past resound,
In hidden chords, our truth is found.
Each moment, captured, drifts away,
Yet through the notes, they always stay.

So let us play, let spirits soar,
In perfect time, forevermore.
The cadence flows, our souls ignite,
Forever wrapped in purest light.

Melodic Memories in Echoing Halls

In the chambers of the past,
Where echoes linger, memories cast.
Footsteps tap on ancient floors,
Each sound a tale that softly shores.

Walls remember whispers sweet,
Melodies where heartbeats meet.
Faint laughter filtered through the years,
A harmony that calms our fears.

Pictures held in twilight's glow,
Moments lost, yet still we know.
Every sigh, a thread of gold,
In stories sung, forever told.

Drifting notes on evening air,
Calling back to what we share.
A melody that pulls us near,
Resonating through the years.

As time unfolds, the music grows,
In every chord, a feeling shows.
We find our place, we stand as one,
In echoes of the setting sun.

Reflections in a Timeless Cadence

In a mirror of the soul's delight,
Moments twinkle, piercing night.
Each reflection tells a tale,
In vibrant hues or shadows pale.

Through shifting dreams, we wander far,
Chasing after every star.
A timeless dance of ebb and flow,
In every heartbeat's steady glow.

Harmonies of what has been,
Blanketing the world within.
Resounding echoes, softly thrum,
As whispered secrets start to hum.

Time stands still in thoughtful gaze,
Illuminating all our days.
In each refrain, a piece displayed,
The rhythm of the life we've made.

So let our hearts align and sing,
For within us, joy takes wing.
In echoes past, we find our way,
A timeless tune that will not sway.

Celestial Chords of Yesteryear

Underneath the vast expanse,
Stars remind us of our dance.
Each twinkle holds a story grand,
Of music played at fate's command.

In cosmic night, we touch the sky,
With melodies that softly fly.
The past inspires our present song,
Guiding notes where we belong.

Harmonies of ages blend,
Across the cosmos, messages send.
A rhythm steady, pulsating light,
Carrying dreams into the night.

With every chord, we feel the pull,
Of yesteryear, a heart so full.
Celestial guidance, ever clear,
In symphonies that draw us near.

So let us strum the heartstrings taut,
With every note, a lesson taught.
In twilight's glow, we raise our voice,
In celestial chords, we rejoice.

Songs of Stardust and Shadows

In the cradle of night, whispers play,
Stars twinkle softly, fading away.
Echoes of dreams in the silver light,
Dance like shadows, lost in the flight.

Every heartbeat carries a sigh,
Underneath the vast, endless sky.
Memories linger, painting the dark,
Fleeting moments leave a spark.

Winds weave tales of love and loss,
Guiding the wanderers, no matter the cost.
Through the cosmos, stories unfold,
In the silence, destinies told.

Shooting stars flicker, love's brief chance,
A cosmic waltz, a fleeting dance.
In twilight's arms, we gently sway,
Finding solace as night turns to day.

Songs of stardust echo so clear,
In the hush of night, we draw near.
Each note a promise, a whispered vow,
In the heart of shadows, we'll sing somehow.

The Infinity of Unheard Chords

In the silence, music plays unseen,
Notes hang in the air, a vibrant sheen.
Time stands still in this hidden embrace,
Where echoes of melodies find their place.

Waves of sound flow like a gentle stream,
Carving through thoughts, a lucid dream.
Each chord a promise, a tale untold,
In the infinity, their beauty unfolds.

A harmony hidden beneath the skin,
Strumming the heart where love can begin.
Unseen symphonies cradle the soul,
Awakening feelings, making us whole.

With each whispered note, a secret shared,
In the unseen realm, emotions bared.
Lost in the rhythm, we drift and float,
On the currents of sound, we learn to gloat.

In shadows we listen, our hearts aligned,
To the music of life, forever intertwined.
The chords remain, though unheard to the ear,
In this symphonic silence, we draw near.

A Chorus in the Wind

Whispers weave through the swaying trees,
Carried by the breath of the soft, cool breeze.
Each leaf joins in with a gentle sigh,
Singing the stories of days gone by.

Clouds drift softly, painting the sky,
As echoes of laughter flutter nearby.
Nature's chorus sings clear and bright,
A symphony hailed by the fading light.

The river hums a soothing tune,
Beneath the watchful, silver moon.
With every ripple, a note aligned,
In the earth's embrace, harmony defined.

Mountains stand tall, guardians grand,
Echoing nature's music across the land.
In the distance, a heartbeat's grace,
Carved by the wind, time's warm embrace.

As dusk descends, the stars ignite,
A chorus of glimmers in the velvet night.
Echoing softly through shadows of time,
In the wind's sweet song, a celestial rhyme.

Strings of Remembrance

From the depths of the heart, memories rise,
Tethered like strings to the vast skies.
With each gentle tug, a past unfolds,
Stories of laughter, secrets untold.

Time plays a tune on this fragile thread,
Binding the living with those now dead.
A tapestry woven from smiles and tears,
Echoes of moments that linger through years.

The strum of a guitar, soft and low,
Calls forth the shadows of long ago.
Each note a memory, vibrant and bright,
Playing the song of lost days and night.

In stillness, we hear the whispers of time,
Notes threading the fabric of reason and rhyme.
Every heartbeat, a reminder we keep,
Strings of remembrance, in silence, we weep.

As we dance through the echoes of what used to be,
We find solace in the strings, setting us free.
Carved into the essence of who we are,
These ties of remembrance guide us like stars.

Reverberations of the Heart

In whispers soft, the echoes sway,
They dance on memories, come what may.
Each heartbeat sings a timeless tune,
Resonating like the light of the moon.

With every pulse, a story told,
Of loves we've lost and dreams of old.
The shadows linger, shadows play,
In reverberations, night and day.

Through gentle sighs, our spirits blend,
With twilight's charm, they twist and bend.
In tender moments, truths ignite,
Reverberations of pure delight.

The heart speaks loud, though lips stay still,
In silent spaces, time stands still.
Each whisper carries, every ache,
In echoes soft, our souls awake.

Lifetimes in Lyrics

In every line, a life unfolds,
A tale of youth, of dreams so bold.
Through verses sung, the years align,
In melodies, our paths entwine.

A chorus bright, where laughter blooms,
In every note, a moment looms.
The rhythm dances, hearts in flight,
Lifetimes in lyrics, pure delight.

With every chord, memories rise,
In harmony beneath the skies.
From sweet refrains to heart's despair,
In every lyric, love laid bare.

Through whispered tones, our dreams converge,
In every song, our souls emerge.
A symphony, both soft and grand,
Lifetimes in lyrics, hand in hand.

Notes Never Forgotten

In faded sheets, the music lies,
Each note a spark that never dies.
With every measure, moments breathe,
In forgotten tunes, we still believe.

The harmony of days gone by,
Resonates beneath the sky.
In silent rooms, the echoes play,
Notes never forgotten, night or day.

Through every chord, our stories blend,
With highs and lows that never end.
A tapestry of joy and sorrow,
In melody, we find tomorrow.

In whispered strains, the past returns,
For every lesson, the heart yearns.
In twilight's hush, our dreams are sought,
In notes never forgotten, love is caught.

Prolonged Harmonies

In tender strains, the echoes bloom,
Where laughter dances, chasing gloom.
Prolonged harmonies rise and fall,
A symphony that binds us all.

Through gentle waves, the music glows,
In every pause, the heart still knows.
In lingering moments, dreams take flight,
Prolonged harmonies, day and night.

With every sound, we draw in close,
A sacred bond, our hearts engrossed.
In every key, our secrets spun,
Prolonged harmonies, two become one.

In whispered tunes, the night unfolds,
In every breath, a tale retold.
Through every note, our souls align,
In prolonged harmonies, love's design.

Eternal Undertones

Whispers of time, soft and low,
Echoes of dreams, where shadows flow,
A gentle touch on the soul's face,
In twilight's arms, we find our place.

Moments linger, like a breath,
Fading slowly, but never death,
Carried forth through nights so long,
In every pulse, we hear the song.

Stars above, they blink and sway,
Guiding us through night and day,
Each heartbeat sings a silent tune,
In the quiet, we find the moon.

A symphony of heartbeats blend,
To timeless rhythms that never end,
In shadows cast by memory's glow,
Eternal undertones still flow.

The world may change, yet we remain,
In life's vast sea, we bear the strain,
Through every joy, and every tear,
Eternal undertones always near.

Melodic Shadows

In the night, a tune takes flight,
Carved from whispers, soft and light,
Dancing 'neath the silver glow,
Melodic shadows gently flow.

Strings of silence, vibrating deep,
Echoes linger, dreams to keep,
Lost in moments that swiftly drift,
Where shadows blend, our spirits lift.

Chasing notes through time and space,
Finding solace in their grace,
As the stars sing songs untold,
Melodic shadows, ever bold.

Harmony of night and day,
Guide the heart along the way,
With every turn, a chance to see,
The magic of how sweet life can be.

In the quiet, we shall find,
The melody that binds mankind,
In whispers low, let it unfold,
Melodic shadows, bright and bold.

Fleeting Yet Lasting

Moments slip through time's embrace,
Yet linger in a sacred space,
Like petals falling from a tree,
Fleeting yet lasting, wild and free.

Time dances on, with grace it flows,
Woven into the heart that knows,
Memories glimmer in our mind,
Fleeting yet lasting, sweetly kind.

In laughter shared, and tears we weep,
Life's essence, in its depth, we keep,
A tapestry of joy and pain,
Fleeting yet lasting, our refrain.

Seasons change, yet love remains,
In every joy and every strain,
A fleeting touch, a lasting kiss,
In time's embrace, we find our bliss.

For every moment that must go,
Leaves behind a timeless glow,
In our hearts, it sings the song,
Fleeting yet lasting, where we belong.

Ballads of the Unheard

In shadows deep, where voices fade,
Reside the tales that time forbade,
A whispered tune, a secret sigh,
Ballads of the unheard, they fly.

Echoes in corners, dark and still,
Yearning hearts, they seek to fill,
Stories waiting to break free,
In silence held, their symphony.

Lost in pages of ancient lore,
Dreamers wander, seeking more,
In every line, a soul laid bare,
Ballads of the unheard, we share.

With every beat, a heartache stirs,
The world may hush, but love confers,
A song emerges from the night,
In quiet moments, it ignites.

For every voice that dared to dream,
In the depths where shadows gleam,
A chorus rises, strong and clear,
Ballads of the unheard, we hear.

Rhythms Carved in the Air

Gentle whispers brush the night,
Dancing shadows take their flight.
Every heartbeat echoes clear,
In the silence, we draw near.

Notes like feathers softly fall,
Carving stories, one and all.
In the breeze, the memories play,
Rhythms guiding us each day.

Stars are twinkling, spirits rise,
Braiding secrets in the skies.
With each pulse, a tune is spun,
Crafting dreams beneath the sun.

In harmonies, we weave our fate,
Timeless moments never wait.
Each breath a note, pure and bright,
Resonates through endless night.

So let the music fill the air,
In every heart, a song we share.
For rhythms carved, in love and care,
Forever linger, everywhere.

Lyrical Legacies of the Past

In dusty pages, tales reside,
Whispers echo, memories guide.
Each stanza holds a timeless grace,
Carving legacies in space.

Voices echo through the years,
Singing laughter, silencing fears.
Every word a treasure true,
Binding hearts with threads anew.

Ballets danced on golden stages,
Remnants found in ancient pages.
Every chorus, every rhyme,
Links the present with the time.

Through tales of love, loss, and fight,
Lyrical echoes take their flight.
In harmony, our spirits blend,
A legacy that will not end.

So gather close, let stories flow,
In whispered lore, we come to know.
These lyrical strands, though worn,
In every heart, they are reborn.

The Melody That Never Quits

In the stillness, a tune awakes,
Like a river, it bends and breaks.
Every note, a step we take,
Through pathways where memories shake.

Strings of joy and threads of pain,
Dance together in soft refrain.
Each moment sings in perfect time,
Climbing high, like mountains we climb.

Through the valleys, echoes flow,
A melody that continues to grow.
Every heartbeat plays a part,
Resounding deep within the heart.

When shadows loom and hope feels slight,
The melody will shine so bright.
In every struggle, find your part,
For the song lives in each heart.

So sing along, let voices rise,
In harmony beneath the skies.
For the melody that never quits,
Guides our souls through all the fits.

Eternal Verses in Stillness

In the calm, where dreams reside,
Eternal verses choose to hide.
Whispers woven in the night,
Break the silence, bring to light.

Each word a brush, painting skies,
A tapestry where silence lies.
In stillness, stories intertwine,
Creating magic, divine design.

Time stands still, as moments flow,
Eternal verses gently grow.
In every pause, a thought takes flight,
Illuminating the heart's true light.

With every breath, a truth unfolds,
In the quiet, a soul beholds.
Embrace the stillness, dwell within,
For eternal verses may begin.

So hold your breath, let silence speak,
In every moment, listen deep.
For in the stillness, life reveals,
Eternal verses, timeless seals.

Time's Unfading Tune

In shadows deep, memories play,
Moments dance in soft array.
Whispers of the past unfold,
A melody of stories told.

Seasons change, yet still we find,
Echoes of love, intertwined.
Each tick of time, a heart's embrace,
Fleeting dreams we can't replace.

In quiet nights, the stars align,
Rhythms of life, a sacred sign.
The pulse of ages, strong and clear,
Time's unfading tune, always near.

With every dawn, new notes arise,
Promises weave beneath the skies.
In every breath, a song reborn,
The tapestry of life, adorned.

Beneath the sky, the ages span,
In harmony, we understand.
As time goes on, we learn to play,
The melody of yesterday.

Ancestral Anthems

In the roots of earth, stories lie,
Whispered tales of days gone by.
Voices echo, strong and brave,
Carrying our legacy to save.

Through ancient woods, the spirits roam,
Guiding hearts that seek a home.
Songs of ancestry, rich and vast,
Binding futures with echoes of the past.

Faces fade, but names remain,
Carved in love, through joy and pain.
We sing the anthems borne of right,
Illuminated by ancestral light.

Together we stand, hand in hand,
Echoes forming a timeless band.
The strength of many, within us flows,
In ancestral echoes, our spirit grows.

With every beat, we honor and tread,
Honoring the paths of those who led.
Ancestral anthems, fierce and bright,
Guide our souls to the endless night.

In the Key of Continuity

Life unfolds in gentle paces,
In the rhythm, time embraces.
Notes of joy, they intertwine,
In the key of love, we find the sign.

Each moment flows, a stream of grace,
Carved by shadows, time can't erase.
Together we rise, then gently fall,
In each crescendo, we hear the call.

With every heartbeat, life's refrain,
Lessons learned, through joy and pain.
In harmony, we weave our tune,
A symphony beneath the moon.

Transitions come, like tides that roll,
In the music, we find our soul.
A dance of dreams, both bold and free,
In the key of continuity.

Together, we write the verses played,
Eternal echoes, never to fade.
In life's grand opus, we find our part,
Composed with love, a steadfast heart.

Verses of Survival

In the face of storms, we stand strong,
Through trials faced, we find our song.
Each struggle, a note in the score,
Verses of survival forevermore.

With every tear, a lesson learned,
In every heart, a fire burns.
Resilience blooms in the harshest ground,
In darkness, new strength is found.

Echoes of courage fill the air,
In whispered hopes, we find repair.
The rhythm of life, a steady beat,
United in purpose, we shall not retreat.

From ashes rise, like phoenix flight,
In the shadows, we find the light.
Every heartbeat, a battle cried,
In verses of survival, we confide.

Together we stand, unyielding, bright,
Chasing dreams through the longest night.
In the tapestry of life, we strive,
We dance through the storms, we are alive.

Songs of Longing

In the heart where shadows dwell,
Whispers float, a soft farewell.
Lonesome stars in velvet night,
Searching for a spark of light.

Echoes of dreams lost in time,
Silent wishes weave a rhyme.
Every sigh a note we cast,
Yearning for the love that passed.

Through the tears, a melody,
Carried by the moonlit sea.
Each wave sings a tender tune,
Longing for the golden moon.

Beneath the trees that bend and sway,
A symphony of night and day.
The wind carries sweet refrains,
Of hopes that blossom despite pains.

In the dusk, a voice outflows,
From broken hearts that love bestows.
A harmony of joy and grief,
In every note, a brief belief.

An Echo in the Silence

When night falls, shadows creep,
In stillness where shadows weep.
Voices lost in time's embrace,
Whisper memories we can trace.

In each heartbeat, a soft sound,
An echo, a love profound.
Through the void, the silence calls,
A haunting tune, in silence falls.

Yet in quiet, thoughts take flight,
Chasing dreams into the night.
Soft reflections, gently drawn,
In the stillness, hope is born.

As stars shimmer above so bright,
Their glow transforms the harvest light.
In that space where echoes fade,
A symphony of love is made.

From shadows, whispers dare to break,
In silence, hearts begin to ache.
But amidst the quiet tones we find,
A rhythm that unites mankind.

Cycles of Sound

In the morning, birds awake,
With melodies they softly make.
Each note dances in the breeze,
A harmony that finds its ease.

Throughout the day, the world hums,
A vibrant tune that softly comes.
From laughter to the bustling streets,
Each echo in the heart repeats.

At dusk, the whispers start to play,
In fading light, they drift away.
The twilight serenades the fields,
With secrets that the night reveals.

When moonlight bathes the earth in glow,
The silenced sounds begin to flow.
In dreams, the cycles intertwine,
Each heartbeat marking time's design.

A sweet refrain that ebbs and swells,
In every note, a story tells.
Life's rhythm guides our feet along,
In cycles of sound, we belong.

Unseen Arias

In shadows deep, their whispers rise,
Unseen echoes in disguise.
A melody, soft and rare,
Floating gently through the air.

Each note, a sigh, a breath unspun,
A song of battles lost and won.
Invisible strings that bind the heart,
Crafting beauty from the dark.

As twilight falls, a hush descends,
With unseen voices where time bends.
These arias, where feelings bloom,
In silence, we discern their tune.

With every heartbeat, we can hear,
The soft crescendo drawing near.
In every shadow, music waits,
In quiet doors that love creates.

So let the unseen sing their song,
In hidden depths where we belong.
A symphony that gently sways,
Through night's embrace, our spirits raise.

Notes of a Shattered Silence

In the stillness, whispers creep,
Fragments of dreams no longer keep.
Echoes dance in the empty air,
A haunting song of deep despair.

Shadows linger, dimly cast,
Memories fading, fading fast.
Hushed sobs mingle with the night,
As silence shatters, seeks the light.

Voices lost in the dark embrace,
Searching for a familiar face.
Each note a puzzle, torn apart,
A melody stitched with a broken heart.

Refrains ripple through the void,
Moments once cherished, now destroyed.
Yet in the cracks, a glimmer shines,
A promise of hope that intertwines.

Beneath the pain, a pulse of grace,
Resilience blooms in this sacred place.
From shattered silence, music grows,
A symphony of life that still flows.

The Ballad of Sunrises and Stars

In the dawn, a canvas spreads,
Colors mingle, life ahead.
Golden light breaks through the gray,
Whispers of a brand new day.

Stars retreat in the waning night,
Guiding dreams to take their flight.
Each sunrise tells a tale untold,
Of warmth and wonder, bold and gold.

Morning dew on petals cling,
Hopes rise like the songs we sing.
Nature's chorus fills the skies,
Harmony where beauty lies.

As twilight falls and shadows creep,
Stars awaken from their sleep.
They twinkle soft in velvety hue,
A serenade for the night anew.

In the dance of both light and dark,
Life unfolds, ignites a spark.
This ballad echoes, near and far,
Of sunrises bright and endless stars.

Unwritten Songs of Forgotten Souls

In corners where the shadows dwell,
Whispers linger, stories tell.
Silent ghosts, the past recalls,
Each moment, like a curtain falls.

Pages blank, as if in wait,
For tales of love, for tales of fate.
Lost echoes flicker in the mind,
Unwritten songs that time unbinds.

Forgotten dreams on dusty shelves,
Hearts that yearned, now silent elves.
Yet in the stillness, voices rise,
Their melodies weave through the skies.

Time weaves threads of silver light,
Reviving stories lost from sight.
With every breath, they seek to be,
The songs of souls that longed to see.

So let us listen, let us write,
To honor those who took their flight.
In unwritten songs, we find our role,
Connecting with each forgotten soul.

Reverberations Through Time's Corridor

Time flows gently, a river wide,
Echoes linger, nowhere to hide.
Footsteps measured, shadows cast,
Memories call from the distant past.

Through corridors of ages gone,
Whispers dance in the breaking dawn.
Stories woven in threads of gold,
Echoes of truths, both brave and bold.

The clock ticks softly, a heartbeat's sway,
Guiding us through night and day.
Each second carries, rich and deep,
The dreams we hold and secrets we keep.

In every moment, candles burn,
Lessons learned, as pages turn.
Reverberations of joy and pain,
In the silent spaces, we remain.

So walk the path, let time unfold,
Embrace the stories yet untold.
For in this corridor, life's design,
Resonates in every line.

Resonance of Forgotten Voices

In shadows where whispers lie,
Memories dance and softly cry.
Lost echoes drift through the night,
Carrying tales of lost light.

Faded songs on the breeze,
Whirling through the ancient trees.
Unheard lyrics still remain,
Haunting the mind with sweet pain.

Each note a ghost from the past,
A fleeting moment, never last.
Binding us to what we've known,
In silence, seeds of love are sown.

The heart remembers every thread,
A tapestry of words once said.
In the quiet, voices blend,
A melody that will not end.

Resonance in the stillness found,
In the echoes, we are bound.
A chorus of the old and new,
In forgotten voices, truth breaks through.

Chasing the Ghost of Melody

In a world where silence reigns,
I wander through the soft refrains.
Chasing shadows of sweet sound,
In hidden corners, lost and found.

A fleeting whisper calls my name,
Through the mist, it burns like flame.
Notes that flutter, out of reach,
The ghost of songs, they softly teach.

I run through fields of fading light,
With every heartbeat, I take flight.
Sifting through the autumn leaves,
Searching for what my heart believes.

The winds carry a tune so far,
Like a hint of a distant star.
Each echo pulls me from the dark,
To find the heart's remaining spark.

In shadows, where the echoes play,
I chase the ghost that will not stay.
A serenade that haunts my soul,
Within this chase, I become whole.

An Endless Ballad of the Heart

Beneath the sky, a story unfolds,
Of love and loss, of dreams retold.
Each heartbeat sings a gentle tune,
A ballad cradled by the moon.

Whispers linger in twilight's breath,
Binding life and love to death.
A rhythm flowing through our veins,
In every joy, in every pain.

With every dawn, a new refrain,
Awakening hope in gentle rain.
A chorus born from every tear,
An endless song, forever near.

Through seasons changing, hearts entwine,
In every echo, love's design.
A tapestry of warmth and grace,
In every heartbeat, find our place.

And when the silence calls my name,
I'll sing this ballad, just the same.
In every note that leaves the heart,
An endless song, we'll never part.

The Dance of Echoed Beats

When twilight falls, the music sways,
To rhythms of forgotten days.
In shadows, beats begin to rise,
A dance beneath the starry skies.

Each pulse a step, each breath a turn,
In this embrace, our passions burn.
Hearts synchronized in timeless flow,
In echoed beats, our spirits grow.

A symphony of whispered dreams,
Where every note endlessly gleams.
With every leap, we touch the sky,
In twilight's glow, we learn to fly.

As night unfolds, we move as one,
To the cadence of the moon and sun.
In this dance, we find our place,
Two souls converging, love's embrace.

So let us twirl through the moonlight's haze,
In the dance of life, our hearts ablaze.
Echoed beats resonate so sweet,
In every step, our lives complete.

The Lifeblood of Unfading Riffs

Guitar strings weave a tale so bright,
Notes dance together, pure delight.
Every strum paints skies of blue,
Melodies alive, ever new.

In shadows of night, the sound ignites,
Weaving through dreams, igniting lights.
Rhythms pulse like a beating heart,
In every soul, they leave their mark.

Lost in a haze of musical stars,
Boundless journeys, near and far.
A symphony wrapped in twilight's embrace,
Music's warmth, a sacred space.

Echoes linger, stories unfold,
The lifeblood of dreams, daring and bold.
Strings tug at memories held tight,
In every riff, we find our light.

Harmonized Moments Suspended in Time

In whispers of dawn, moments freeze,
Time dances gently among the trees.
Melodies curl like morning mist,
Each heartbeat a note, too pure to resist.

Stars hum softly in twilight's glow,
Capturing dreams, allowing them to flow.
A chorus of memories intertwines,
Suspended in frames, like timeless designs.

Colors blend in a vibrant hue,
Brushstrokes of life, forever true.
Harmony nestled in every sigh,
Fragile and strong, we reach for the sky.

With every heartbeat, we create,
Moments that linger, never too late.
In the tapestry woven, love's the thread,
Harmonized dreams that never shed.

Chorus of the Undying Heart

In the silence, a whisper calls,
Every heartbeat, the music enthralls.
Resonating deep, the echoes start,
A chorus sung from the undying heart.

Through valleys low and mountains high,
Feel the surge as spirits fly.
Songs of courage, joy, and pain,
In every note, love's refrain.

Through storms that threaten, shadows that creep,
The melody rises, promises keep.
A symphony crafted by hands unseen,
Binding our souls in harmonies keen.

In every challenge, a rhythm found,
The dance of life, a sacred sound.
With open hearts, we take our part,
Singing along to the undying heart.

Tides of Echoed Reflections

Waves crash softly on ancient shores,
Carrying whispers of forgotten lore.
Each ripple reveals a secret lost,
Tides of time, we pay the cost.

In mirrored waters, stories play,
Reflections of night, intriguingly sway.
Embracing shadows in rhythmic flow,
Where memories linger, thoughts bestow.

With every crest, a longing sigh,
Seeking answers from the sky.
The ocean breathes, the heart explores,
In echoed reflections, peace restores.

Nature's chorus, ever profound,
In breathless silence, we are found.
Through tides that pull, and dreams that soar,
We embrace the echoes on the shore.

Notes Worn by Time's Passage

In the quiet of old halls,
Faded notes whisper tales,
Each chord a memory,
Time's hand gently trails.

Dusty pages turn slow,
Fragrant ink lingers near,
Echoes of laughter,
Resonant with cheer.

Moments captured in sound,
Fractured yet so whole,
Notes worn by the years,
Sing deep to the soul.

Shadows cling to the light,
In melodies, they bind,
Time writes on the silence,
What's lost, we still find.

Each strum, a heartbeat,
Each pause, a sigh,
In the dance of time's flow,
These notes never die.

The Continuum of Silent Songs

In the hush of the night,
Where shadows softly play,
Songs linger unspoken,
In a harmonious sway.

Stars blink in the dark,
A symphony of dreams,
Echoes of the cosmos,
Are more than they seem.

Whispers of the unknown,
In the void they resound,
Across the endless ages,
Silent songs abound.

Time bends to the rhythm,
As echoes intertwine,
Carried by the stillness,
Each note, a lifeline.

In the heart of the night,
Where silence holds its throne,
The continuum whispers,
You are never alone.

Celestial Tones of Discovery

In the vastness of space,
New melodies arise,
Celestial tones ignite,
Beneath ever-changing skies.

Galaxies twirl and spin,
In a dance so divine,
Harmony in motion,
In the great cosmic line.

Shooting stars bring notes,
A symphony so bright,
Every twinkle a spark,
Illuminates the night.

Discoveries await,
In the silent expanse,
The universe hums softly,
Inviting us to dance.

With each cosmic heartbeat,
Wonders unfold unfurled,
Celestial tones of hope,
Embrace the waiting world.

Harmonies that Dance Beyond

In the realm of the unseen,
Harmonies take flight,
Dancing on the edges,
Of day slipping to night.

Whispers weave through the air,
A tapestry so bright,
Each thread a note of love,
In the softest light.

Beyond what the eye meets,
A world of sound exists,
Tunes that sway and ripple,
In a magical mist.

Across the tides of time,
In every heart they sing,
Harmonies that resonate,
In the warmth of spring.

With every step we take,
Melodies are drawn,
Harmonies that dance,
To the break of dawn.

The Symphony of Life's Remnants

In whispers soft, the echoes roam,
Across the paths of dreams once sown.
Each note, a tale of joy and strife,
Composing the symphony of life.

Beneath the stars, the shadows play,
Carving memories that will not fray.
Each heartbeat sings, each breath a rhyme,
A melody entwined with time.

From laughter's peak to sorrow's fall,
In every rise, we hear the call.
The stages shift, the players change,
Yet, through it all, we feel the range.

In quiet moments, truths unfold,
Hidden stories waiting to be told.
Life's remnants linger, sweet and deep,
In the symphony, our spirits leap.

So let us dance to every sound,
In harmony, our souls unbound.
For in this piece, we find our place,
A timeless waltz through vastness' grace.

Chords of Time Unveiled

In the silence, secrets weave,
Through chords of time, we learn to believe.
Each strum a thread, each note a cry,
Songs of the ages drift and fly.

With every heartbeat, pulses grow,
A rhythmic dance in twilight's glow.
The past and present intertwine,
Crafting futures in every line.

Echoes of laughter, whispers of pain,
In the tapestry of joy and rain.
Every heartstrings' pull and sway,
Reveal the truth in night and day.

As we unravel what lies beneath,
New horizons rise from layered sheath.
Chords of memories, bright and pale,
In the song of life, we set our sail.

So let the music guide our way,
In every moment, in every play.
For time unveils its wondrous reach,
Each chord a lesson, each note a teach.

Elysian Warmth in Every Note

In distant realms where echoes dwell,
A harmony cast under a spell.
Every note a whisper, soft and sweet,
Elysian warmth, a tender meet.

With every chord, the heart ignites,
Dancing shadows in the twilight lights.
Melodies weave through the fabric of night,
Filling empty spaces with pure delight.

The symphony flows like rivers clear,
Each drop of sound, a song sincere.
In every pause, the world stands still,
Breathless moments, a longing thrill.

The universe hums in perfect sync,
Stirring the soul, making hearts link.
In each refrain, love's essence glows,
Elysian warmth in life's great prose.

So let us revel in this embrace,
With every note, we find our place.
In music's cradle, hope takes flight,
Transforming darkness into light.

Timeless Waltz of Wandering Souls

In endless dance, we twirl and sway,
Through realms where light meets shadow play.
Every step unfolds a tale anew,
In the waltz of souls, we are true.

Lost in the rhythm of fate's design,
Guided by stars that brightly shine.
Our footsteps echo in life's sweet grace,
As we find solace in every space.

In timeless whispers, we hear the call,
As wandering hearts embrace it all.
Every encounter, a fleeting kiss,
In the dance of existence, we find bliss.

With laughter and tears, we all belong,
In the sacred bond of life's great song.
Each soul a thread, woven tight,
Creating beauty in the night.

So let us waltz through the cosmic swirl,
In the circle of life, let our spirits unfurl.
Timeless moments, hand in hand,
Together we wander in this vast land.

The Remnant of Unbroken Chords

In shadows where the silence dwells,
A whisper of forgotten bells.
The echoes call in twilight's breath,
Remnants linger, defying death.

Across the fields where dreams once flew,
The music waits, a tender hue.
Each note a thread in time's embrace,
A tapestry of songs we trace.

The chords remain, though voices fade,
In every pause, in every shade.
The heart recalls what once was bright,
A melody draped in the night.

When stars align and shadows blend,
The unbroken rhythms comprehend.
In hushed refrain and fleeting start,
The harmony lives in every heart.

So let us strum with gentle hands,
The secrets known in silent lands.
For even lost, the music stays,
An ageless song that never frays.

Lyrics That Linger Through Ages

Whispers ride the winds of time,
In verses etched, a silent rhyme.
Words that dance on memory's stage,
Lyrics penned on history's page.

Through ancient halls, the echoes roam,
In every heart, they find a home.
In fireside tales and moonlit nights,
The verses glow with gentle lights.

They sing of love and tales of woe,
Of journeys vast, of rivers slow.
In every soul, they weave their thread,
From dawn's first light, to dusk's soft bed.

A chorus shared by young and old,
In every story, new and bold.
The lyrics linger, soft yet grand,
An anthem sung across the land.

So let the echoes never cease,
In every heart, may songs find peace.
For as long as time can recall,
The lyrics hold us, one and all.

Melodies Adrift in Memory's Sea

In tides that ebb, in waves that flow,
The melodies rise, a soft glow.
Each note a sail on waters wide,
Drifting through dreams where secrets hide.

With every breath, the echoes sway,
A current pulls the night to day.
In whispered tones that shape the air,
The songs of life weave everywhere.

Past shores where time forgot to tread,
The symphony of thoughts unsaid.
In gentle ripples, lost and found,
The melodies hum without a sound.

Through storms that crash and clouds that part,
The music journeys, close to heart.
It travels far, yet feels so near,
A timeless tune that draws us here.

So let the waves embrace our soul,
In memory's sea, we find our role.
For every note that slips away,
Leaves traces in the light of day.

Cadences of the Unseen Past

In echoes faint, the past will play,
With cadences that softly sway.
The stories etched in dusk and dawn,
In every heart, the echoes drawn.

Whispers linger in the air,
A dance of shadows everywhere.
Each step recalls where we have been,
In silent halls, what might have seen.

The rhythm flows like ancient streams,
In every thought, in every dream.
The past unfolds with gentle might,
A symphony hidden from sight.

And when the night enfolds the day,
The hidden notes begin to sway.
In quiet moments, truths will glean,
The cadences of what has been.

So listen close, the past will sing,
In every flutter, every wing.
For time's embrace can never part,
The music played within the heart.

Melodies Forged in Transience

Whispers dance upon the breeze,
Softly fading with each sigh.
In shadows where the sunlight flees,
Moments linger, then they die.

Notes of laughter drift away,
Like petals in a summer sun.
Echoes of the joy they play,
In the heart, they weigh a ton.

Time, elusive, bends and sways,
Carving paths in fading light.
Memories weave through endless days,
Yet dim with every dusk in sight.

Chords that bind us start to break,
As seasons blur with changing hue.
In every heart a tender ache,
A song of what we thought we knew.

But still, the melodies we hold,
Are treasures wrapped in fragile dreams.
In stories, yet to be retold,
The essence of our laughter gleams.

A Lament for Lost Chords

In silent rooms where shadows weep,
The echoes of a song remain.
Each note a memory, buried deep,
In anguish, we recall the pain.

Breathed life into a fleeting sound,
We played our verses, hearts in tune.
Now silence bridges all the ground,
Lamenting nights beneath the moon.

Fingers dance upon the strings,
Yet find no joy in what's amiss.
A haunting whisper softly clings,
To empty spaces, void of bliss.

Time steals harmonies away,
Replacing music with the hush.
In every chord, a price we pay,
Wishing for the vibrant rush.

But even in our deepest grief,
There's warmth within the bitter ache.
In loss, we find a sweet relief,
A song reborn from love we make.

The Timeless Waltz of Remembrance

Two souls entwined in twilight's glow,
They dance to rhythms worn with time.
The pulse of memories ebb and flow,
In every step, a whispered rhyme.

The floor beneath, a tapestry,
Of laughter, tears, and fleeting foes.
With every spin, shadows agree,
That love is where the heart still grows.

Years may pass like fleeting dreams,
Yet in their eyes, the world ignites.
A truth that stirs the gentle streams,
As stars awaken in the nights.

With every twirl, the past aligns,
In echoes that the heart retains.
Together still, through aged signs,
The dance of life forever reigns.

So let us waltz, and never part,
In timeless rhythm, hand in hand.
For in each beat, we find our heart,
A symphony from love, so grand.

Ethereal Echoes of Life's Tune

In whispers soft as morning mist,
Life's melody begins to play.
With every breath, a fleeting twist,
A tapestry of night and day.

The laughter of a child at play,
The rustle of the autumn leaves,
In every note, a sweet bouquet,
Reminds us how the spirit weaves.

Seasons change, like flowing streams,
Moments cherished, swiftly pass.
In time's embrace, we find our dreams,
Reflections held in crystal glass.

Yet in the quiet, echoes sing,
Of journeys paved with love and light.
Each heartbeat feels the joy it brings,
In harmony, we take our flight.

So let us dance, and feel alive,
In every instant, grace unfolds.
For life's sweet tune will always thrive,
In hearts where beauty's story holds.

Resonant Recollections of a Faded Past

In shadows deep, where whispers dwell,
Old memories ring like a distant bell.
Fleeting images, soft and slight,
Dance through the corridors of night.

Faded pictures, sepia tones,
Echoes of laughter, a child's soft groans.
Time weaves stories, gentle and vast,
In every heartbeat, a glimpse of the past.

Moonlight kisses the dusty frame,
Each face a note, each word a name.
Dreams once woven, now frayed and thin,
Yet in the silence, they quietly spin.

Through rusted gates, lost voices call,
In hidden corners, we stumble and fall.
Amidst the ruins, we seek what remains,
The ghost of a love that forever sustains.

With every sigh, the heartstrings tug,
A tapestry woven with each soft hug.
In this maze of time, we wander, we roam,
Finding our way, always returning home.

An Overture to Lost Moments

Softly the winds carry whispers away,
Echoes of laughter that danced in the day.
Moments like petals, drifting on air,
Fragile and fleeting, yet vivid and rare.

Beneath the old oak, promises made,
In sun-kissed afternoons, dreams never fade.
Time played its tune in a sweet serenade,
Each note a memory, tenderly laid.

Fragments of joy in the stillness abide,
Through tear-streaked faces, we learn to confide.
Purposeful paths where the heartbeats collide,
An overture's grace, in love we're tied.

Faded horizons hold stories untold,
Moments like treasures, more precious than gold.
In the hush of twilight, reflections take flight,
A canvas of life painted soft in the night.

With each passing hour, the past lingers near,
Bathing in echoes that whisper, "I'm here."
An overture written in sighs and in hopes,
As we navigate life on this delicate slope.

Chronicles of Timeless Serenades

Beneath the starry quilt of night,
Sweet melodies flow, taking flight.
Each note, a whisper, a story to share,
Chronicles kept in the cool evening air.

Moments of solace in the gentle breeze,
Harmony sings in the swaying trees.
Time weaves its tapestry with threads of sound,
In echoes of love, our hearts are unbound.

The moon takes stage, casting a glow,
Illuminating paths where shadows once flowed.
A dance of yesterdays, unfolding anew,
In timeless serenades, life's rhythm is true.

Forgotten tunes in the dusk gleam bright,
Revealing lost stories in the silence of night.
With every heartbeat, past and present blend,
In chronicles spoken that never quite end.

Here, in the stillness, we gather, we cling,
To melodies borne on the breath of the spring.
When whispers of time meld with love's gentle aim,
We find in the music, we're all part of the same.

Lifelines of Forgotten Melodies

In the heart of silence, the echoes awake,
Forgotten melodies, a path they take.
Wandering notes in the twilight glow,
A symphony of whispers that softly flow.

Through dusty old albums, faintly they call,
Familiar refrains, resonating small.
Each chord a journey, a glimpse into light,
A tapestry woven in the cover of night.

The laughter of children, a songbird's cheer,
Fleeting moments we hold most dear.
Memory's canvas, painted in hues,
Of lifelines stitched through the old and the new.

With every heartbeat, lost notes reveal,
The music of moments that time cannot steal.
In laughter and tears, our heartstrings entwine,
Lifelines of memories, forever divine.

So let the world sing its soft serenade,
In spaces between, where joy won't fade.
For every lost melody finds its true form,
In the lifelines we cherish, forever to warm.

Notes Woven Through Eternity

In whispers soft, the echoes play,
Each note a thread of night and day.
They weave a tale of time, divine,
A melody where stars align.

Through ancient woods, the songbirds call,
Their harmonies in twilight fall.
Each fleeting sound, a moment's grace,
Etched in the heart, time can't erase.

A river flows with gentle ease,
Carrying dreams on its breeze.
The symphony of life unfolds,
In every heartbeat, stories told.

When silence falls, and shadows grow,
The music lingers, soft and slow.
In every space where echoes meet,
A timeless dance, a pulse of beat.

Eternal notes, forever spun,
Woven threads, our lives as one.
In every breath, in every sigh,
The song remains; it will not die.

The Spirit of Unyielding Lyrics

In the realm of unspoken dreams,
The spirit flows, or so it seems.
With every line, the heart ignites,
Unyielding words in endless flights.

Through valleys deep and mountains high,
Lyrics whisper, never shy.
Each verse a dawn, each chorus bright,
In shadows cast, they spark the light.

The rhythm pulses in the veins,
In love's embrace, no room for chains.
A testament to strength and care,
With every breath, the world lays bare.

Like rivers carving through the stone,
Each lyric speaks; we are not alone.
Their echoes rise, defying time,
In harmony, forever rhyme.

With fervent hope, the songs we sing,
In battles fought, they give us wings.
The spirit bold, our voices soar,
Unyielding hearts forever more.

Undying Harmonies in Fading Light

As daylight wanes, soft shadows grow,
Harmonies of dusk, a gentle flow.
In whispers sweet, the night unfolds,
Undying tunes, a tale retold.

While stars ignite the velvet sky,
The melodies begin to fly.
Each note a spark, a fleeting hope,
In fading light, we learn to cope.

A lullaby for dreams anew,
In twilight's grasp, the heart stays true.
The world transforms with every chord,
In quiet moments, we're restored.

In shadows deep, where silence thrives,
The undying song of love survives.
It dances softly, sings its plight,
In echoes held, we find our light.

Through the hourglass, time does weave,
An ageless bond that won't deceive.
In the twilight's glow, we find our way,
Harmonies that forever stay.

A Symphony Beyond Departure

As journeys start, horizons call,
A symphony awaits us all.
In every step, each path we take,
Beyond departure, dreams awake.

With every heartbeat, music grows,
A tapestry of highs and lows.
Through laughter bright, through tears we share,
A melody lingers in the air.

When seasons change, and days are long,
The echoes fade, yet still, we're strong.
A legacy of notes remains,
In every loss, the spirit gains.

With open arms, we greet the end,
Each note a lover, every bend.
In the silence, hear the grace,
A symphony we all embrace.

Though farewells linger in the night,
The music shines, a guiding light.
In every heart, the song is clear,
A symphony that conquers fear.

Ballads Beyond the Horizon

In twilight's glow, the shadows dance,
Whispers of fate in a hopeful trance.
The stars align on the velvet sea,
Guiding the hearts of the wild and free.

Mountains rise, like dreams unchained,
Echoes of laughter, joys uncontained.
Hands held tight against the night,
Together we soar, taking flight.

Each road we walk, a story spun,
No end in sight, just love begun.
The sunset glows, a canvas bright,
Painting our souls with endless light.

Through stormy skies and gentle rain,
We find our strength in joy and pain.
With every note in this sweet refrain,
We chase the dawn where spirits gain.

So sing with me, let voices blend,
In every heartbeat, our souls ascend.
For beyond the horizon, dreams entwine,
In ballads true, our hearts align.

The Unbroken Melody

In silence born, a note takes flight,
A tender sound, the purest light.
Each chord resounds, unspoken grace,
In every heart, it finds its place.

With every pulse, a rhythm flows,
A dance of life, where love bestows.
Through highs and lows, the music plays,
In darkest nights, it lights the way.

The symphony of souls entwined,
In harmony, we seek, we find.
A gentle hum, a sweet caress,
In every heart, this truth we bless.

Through stormy seas and tranquil shores,
The unbroken melody endures.
With every tear, with every cheer,
The song of life forever near.

So let it soar, this timeless song,
In every heart where we belong.
For in the echoes, we remain,
The unbroken melody of pain.

Fluid Echoes

Ripples in water, soft and sweet,
Tell of the journey beneath our feet.
Every heartbeat, a wave on shore,
In fluid echoes, we seek for more.

Breezes carry whispers through the trees,
Calling our dreams on gentle breeze.
Each moment's breath in nature's song,
Guides us onward, where we belong.

The river flows, a path unknown,
In every twist, the seeds are sown.
With every turn, a chance to grow,
In fluid echoes, let love flow.

Cascading waterfalls, voices blend,
In silent pact, we find our friends.
Together strong, we stand as one,
Through fluid echoes, life's never done.

So seek the sound in quiet night,
In every shadow, find the light.
For in the echoes, we'll discover,
The song of life, one heart, one lover.

Soulful Cadences

In every heartbeat, a rhythm sings,
A dance of life, the joy it brings.
With every step, we walk in time,
In soulful cadences, hearts align.

The world spins on, a fleeting phase,
Each day unfolds in vibrant ways.
Through laughter shared and trials faced,
Our soulful journeys interlaced.

From whispered dreams to fiery goals,
The melody of our aching souls.
In shadows cast, in sunlight's glow,
In soulful cadences, we learn and grow.

With every note, emotions rise,
A symphony beneath the skies.
In quiet moments or loud refrains,
Our hearts compose what love sustains.

So join the song, let voices soar,
Together strong, forevermore.
For in these cadences, we find peace,
Our souls in rhythm, never cease.

Chords of the Past

In shadows of time, voices fade,
Memories linger, softly laid.
A strum of nostalgia, whispering light,
Echoes of laughter in the night.

Fragments of music, woven in dreams,
Stories unspoken, unravel at seams.
Each note a reminder, of days gone by,
In the heart of the moment, we live and sigh.

Melodies drift on, with gentle grace,
Guiding us home to a familiar place.
With every chord, the past replays,
A haunting refrain in the twilight haze.

Beneath the stars, we find our way,
The song of the past, a timeless ballet.
Harmony dances, over shadows it sweeps,
In the chords of memory, our spirit keeps.

So let the music play, never cease,
Finding solace in notes, a sweet release.
In the chords of the past, forever we blend,
A tapestry woven, where stories transcend.

Resilience in Refrains

In the tempest's roar, we find our voice,
With each refrain, we make our choice.
Echoes of courage ring loud and clear,
Resilience blooms, banishing fear.

Through trials faced, the heartbeats rise,
In melodies strong, we reach for the skies.
Harmony found in the struggle we share,
United we stand, with love and care.

Verses of hope, like a lighthouse beam,
Guiding us forward, igniting our dream.
With each note struck, we rise and stand tall,
In resilience, we flourish, we never fall.

The struggles behind us, we cast to the sea,
Our spirits uplifted, forever free.
With courage as rhythm, we sing our refrain,
In the heart of the storm, we dance in the rain.

Every whisper of doubt, we turn to gold,
Writing our stories, brave and bold.
In the song of our lives, forever we play,
Resilience in refrains, come what may.

Notes Carried on the Wind

Softly they travel, on breezes so light,
Notes of the past, taking flight.
Whispers of dreams, in the twilight glow,
Carried on currents, where wildflowers grow.

Each melody dances through branches and trees,
Swaying with rhythm, lost in the breeze.
The song of the earth, in harmony sings,
Notes on the wind, like the joy of spring.

Carried to valleys, where rivers do flow,
Echoes of wonder, in sunlight's glow.
In the rustle of leaves, stories unfold,
A tapestry woven, with voices bold.

With the whispers of twilight, dreams start to weave,
Notes on the wind, in which we believe.
Carrying hopes, to horizons afar,
In the symphony shared, we find who we are.

So listen closely, let your heart spin,
To the notes of the world, where our journeys begin.
Carried on breezes, forever entwined,
In the breath of the wind, our spirits aligned.

The Rhythm of Eternity

In the heartbeat of time, we dance and sway,
To the rhythm of life, come what may.
Every moment a pulse, a beat so profound,
In the cadence of ages, our voices surround.

Waves of existence, they rise and they fall,
In harmony's embrace, we answer the call.
With every sunrise, a chance to compose,
A melody crafted, as the world softly glows.

In laughter and sorrow, we find our refrain,
A chorus of souls, in joy and in pain.
The rhythm of eternity echoes so clear,
Binding us together, drawing us near.

As stars leap and twinkle, their dance in the night,
We move hand in hand, in love's gentle light.
In the timbre of memories, our stories entwine,
The rhythm of eternity, forever divine.

So let us embrace every note, every sound,
In the vastness of time, where wonders abound.
For in each heartbeat, we find our infinity,
In the rhythm of life, the essence of we.

Rewind and Resonate

In echoes of dreams, we find our way,
Each moment a thread, that beckons to stay.
Whispers of time, they gently unwind,
As memories linger, in heart, intertwined.

We dance in the shadows of what we once knew,
Holding on tight to the feelings so true.
The past is a melody, softly it plays,
Rewinding the hours of luminous days.

With every heartbeat, we echo the past,
A symphony woven, forever to last.
In the chambers of memory, we carve our tune,
Resonating softly, like night-silvered moon.

The laughter we shared, the tears that we shed,
In rewind we delve, through the words left unsaid.
Moments in time, like fine woven art,
Resonating deeply, the song of the heart.

So let us embrace all we've come to adore,
In the echoes and whispers, we'll find even more.
Rewind and resonate, let love gently flow,
In the dance of our souls, let the memories glow.

Lasting Imprints

Through pathways of time, we walk hand in hand,
Each step leaves a mark, like footprints in sand.
The laughter we shared, in the warmth of the sun,
Lasting imprints recorded, we've only begun.

In shadows of twilight, our secrets remain,
Echoes of whispers, like soft summer rain.
We cherish the moments, the stories we weave,
Lasting impressions, in hearts that believe.

The canvas of life, with colors we blend,
Each hue tells a story, as beginnings descend.
In the gallery of time, our memories shine,
Lasting imprints of love, forever entwined.

With grace we remember, the joy and the strife,
In the book of our souls, we write of our life.
Each chapter a bond, with bold strokes and dare,
Lasting imprints of hope, scattered everywhere.

So here's to the journey, the paths that we roam,
In the heart of each moment, we find our true home.
Lasting imprints of joy, forever will stay,
As shadows of love guide us along the way.

Unwritten Anthems

In the silence of dreams, a song starts to rise,
Unwritten anthems, beneath endless skies.
Notes linger softly, on the edge of our lips,
Waiting for moments, our souls to eclipse.

With every heartbeat, a rhythm unfolds,
An anthem in us, rich stories told.
Verses unspoken, like whispers in flight,
We dance to the echoes, igniting the night.

Through uncharted waters, we sail the unknown,
Our hearts are the vessels, where love has been sown.
The chords of existence, resonate clear,
Unwritten anthems, forever we'll hear.

Each laugh is a chorus, each sigh is a rhyme,
We sing of the moments, transcending all time.
In the tapestry woven, our spirits ignite,
Unwritten anthems, embracing the light.

So raise up your voice, let the world hear your song,
In the symphony of life, we all belong.
Unwritten anthems, waiting to soar,
Together we'll harmonize, forevermore.

Sentiments in Serenade

In the twilight hush, where dreams softly sway,
Sentiments linger, in a serenade's play.
With each note we breathe, love dances anew,
In the gentle embrace, our hearts find their due.

The moonlight reflects, on whispers profound,
Serenading our souls, in rhythms unbound.
We sing of the moments, both tender and bold,
Sentiments captured, more precious than gold.

In the garden of time, where sweet memories bloom,
Each serenade a promise, dispelling all gloom.
The echoes of laughter, like petals take flight,
Sentiments in serenade, glowing so bright.

With harmonies flowing, our wishes take form,
In the heart of the night, love becomes the norm.
We waltz through the verses, together we glide,
Sentiments in serenade, forever our guide.

So let the world listen to our heartfelt refrain,
In the symphony of dreams, there's nothing to feign.
Sentiments in serenade, pure as the dawn,
Together we've crafted, a love that goes on.

Traces of Lost Chords

In shadows where whispers dwell,
Fragments of music softly swell.
Fingers trace an empty space,
Lingering notes lost in grace.

A melody's ghost lingers near,
Fading echoes, sweet and clear.
Harmonies drift through the night,
Seeking the dawn's gentle light.

A symphony lost in the dark,
Each silence, a wistful spark.
Chords that once played now stand still,
Yearning for the voice of will.

Unwritten tales of yesteryears,
Composed of both laughter and tears.
Notes in the air, gently cease,
A longing for bittersweet peace.

Yet in the silence, hope remains,
Music lingers in soft refrains.
Traces of what once was true,
Hold fast to the heart, like dew.

Cadence of Mind and Heart

Thoughts dance lightly on the breeze,
Interwoven with silent pleas.
The rhythm of dreams softly calls,
As time, like a river, gently sprawls.

Hearts beat with a tender tune,
Underneath the pale, swooning moon.
Each heartbeat a note in the air,
Resonating with love and care.

In moments where silence speaks loud,
The pulse of the world, both humble and proud.
Melodies woven with dreams profound,
In every breath, life's beauty is found.

Voices blend in a seamless flow,
Guiding us where we long to go.
Each whisper weaves a story unheard,
A symphony born from the heart's word.

Together, mind and heart align,
Creating cadence, a sacred sign.
In harmony, we find our place,
As life unfolds with bittersweet grace.

Sounds of Solace

Soft echoes of the evening light,
Whispering peace in the falling night.
Gentle winds carry a silent plea,
As stars awaken, wild and free.

The rustle of leaves, a soothing song,
Echoing where the hearts belong.
In this quiet, all fears erase,
Finding comfort in nature's embrace.

Ripples of water, a tender sigh,
Mirroring dreams as they drift by.
In every sound, a chance to heal,
Moments of calm that fate may steal.

Crickets serenade the fading day,
Guiding twilight with their soft play.
Each note, a treasure, a solace found,
In the simplicity of life's sound.

Space to breathe, to rest, to be,
In the language of stillness, we see.
Where sounds of solace intertwine,
A heart at peace, a spirit divine.

Histories in Harmony

In echoes of time, stories reside,
Weaving a tapestry, side by side.
Notes of the past in every heart,
Histories sung, a profound art.

Voices of ages, a chorus strong,
Reminders of where we all belong.
In the fabric of life, threads entwine,
Carrying dreams like vintage wine.

Moments captured, a rhythmic dance,
Lifetimes blended in fate's sweet chance.
Melodies linger, sweet and clear,
Singing the truths, holding them dear.

Legacy flows through every sound,
In the stillness, history's found.
A harmony born from laughter and pain,
Carved in the heart, like gentle rain.

Together we stand, hand in hand,
In the symphony of this vast land.
Histories echo, a timeless call,
Resonating within us, after all.

www.ingramcontent.com/pod-product-compliance
Ingram Content Group UK Ltd.
Pitfield, Milton Keynes, MK11 3LW, UK
UKHW032223171224
452550UK00006B/74